HISTORY OF FUN STUFF

The Superstar Story of the Harlem Globetrotters

by Larry Dobrow
illustrations by Scott Burroughs

Ready-to-Read

Simon Spotlight
New York   London   Toronto   Sydney   New Delhi

SIMON SPOTLIGHT

An imprint of Simon & Schuster Children's Publishing Division • 1230 Avenue of the Americas, New York, New York 10020
This Simon Spotlight edition December 2017 • © 2017 Copyright Harlem Globetrotters International, Inc. All rights reserved, including
the right of reproduction in whole or in part in any form. Photo credits for all photography: Harlem Globetrotters International, Inc.
SIMON SPOTLIGHT, READY-TO-READ, and colophon are registered trademarks of Simon & Schuster, Inc.
For information about special discounts for bulk purchases, please contact Simon & Schuster Special Sales at 1-866-506-1949
or business@simonandschuster.com. Manufactured in the United States of America 1117 LAK • 10 9 8 7 6 5 4 3 2 1
Cataloging-in-Publication Data for this title is available from the Library of Congress.
ISBN 978-1-4814-8749-8 (hc) • ISBN 978-1-4814-8748-1 (pbk) • ISBN 978-1-4814-8750-4 (eBook)

CONTENTS

CHAPTER 1
Way Back in the Day

The Harlem Globetrotters have been sinking jumpers and entertaining fans for so long that they are one of the world's most recognizable sports teams. But even a team this famous had to start somewhere and grow into what they are today.
So how did the Harlem Globetrotters come to be, and what incredible feats has this team accomplished in nearly one hundred years? By the time you finish reading this book, you will know the answer to these questions and many more! You will be a History of Fun Stuff Expert on the Harlem Globetrotters!

A whole lot of stuff happened in 1926. The first-ever public showing of a television took place when Scottish inventor John Logie Baird displayed his "televisor" to scientists and reporters. The Great Miami Hurricane swept through southern Florida with winds of one hundred fifty miles per hour and a ten-foot storm surge from the ocean. That's more than a foot higher than the tallest person recorded in history: Robert Pershing Wadlow, who was measured at eight feet eleven inches tall.

As for basketball, in 1926 the sport had been around for thirty-five years. It was founded in 1891 by gym teacher James Naismith. At that time basketball didn't even feature nets and backboards. The game was originally played by shooting the ball into peach baskets!

In Chicago, in 1926 and 1927, an African American basketball team began to play around the city. They soon became known as the Savoy Big Five because they played at the Savoy Ballroom. The owners of the ballroom thought a basketball game would be a great way to get people to come to their venue and stay after the game. When some of the players, including Tommy Brookins and Inman Jackson, left the team, they formed a new squad, known as the Globe Trotters. Around that time, a man named Abe Saperstein began to schedule games for the team.

Legend has it that soon after they were formed, the team played its first road game on January 27, 1927, in Hinckley, Illinois—a town about fifty miles outside Chicago. As time went on, Abe Saperstein began to coach the team in addition to finding players, designing uniforms, and subbing in when necessary.

Tommy Brookins

Inman Jackson

Abe Saperstein

Even in their early days, the players
from Chicago had the name of a
different city stitched on the front of
their jerseys: New York. Confused?
To convince fans that this squad was
more than just a bunch of local players,
Saperstein switched names three or four
times during the team's first decade.
They were, depending on the day
you happened to catch up with them,
Saperstein's New York Globe Trotters,
Saperstein's Harlem Globe Trotters, or
the Original Harlem N.Y. Globe Trotters.
Harlem was chosen as the team's
"home" due to the increasing fame of
that New York City neighborhood. The
Harlem Renaissance of the 1920s and
1930s saw tremendous achievements
in the art, literature, and music
made by African Americans living
and working in Harlem. A number
of influential musicians, writers, and

artists called Harlem home during the period, including singer Billie Holiday; composer and pianist Duke Ellington; novelist, poet, and playwright Langston Hughes; and novelist Zora Neale Hurston.

Globetrotters stuck as the team name
because it suggested, if a bit misleadingly,
that the players had performed on courts
all over the world. (As we'll see later, the

team didn't play overseas until the 1950s.) But by the late 1940s it was settled: Saperstein's squad would be known forevermore as the Harlem Globetrotters. From these beginnings, the Harlem Globetrotters set off to live up to their name. But first, they would permanently change the idea of what a professional sports team could be—and in doing so, become the first one to emphasize entertainment as much as it did athleticism. As a result, the Globetrotters' influence can be felt in organizations as diverse as today's National Football League (NFL) and World Wrestling Entertainment (WWE).

CHAPTER 2
Breaking Down Barriers

The impact of the Harlem Globetrotters went far beyond the court. The Globetrotters won their first World Basketball Championship in 1940—with a roster featuring five African American starters. At that time many sports leagues in America were segregated by race. That means that leagues like the NBA (National Basketball Association) did not allow African American players on the teams. When the Globetrotters defeated the Minneapolis Lakers and George "Mr. Basketball" Mikan in 1948 and 1949, their display of skill and athleticism helped accelerate the addition of African American players to the NBA.

In 1950, Globetrotter Nathaniel "Sweetwater" Clifton became the first African American basketball player to sign a contract to play in the NBA, joining the New York Knicks that season.

Nathaniel "Sweetwater" Clifton

The Harlem Globetrotters helped break down other barriers as well. In 1985, Olympic gold medalist (and future member of the Naismith Memorial Basketball Hall of Fame) Lynette Woodard joined the team, the first of fifteen female Globetrotters. The visibility of female Globetrotters has helped pave the way for women's professional sports teams like those of the Women's National Basketball Association (WNBA).

In 1993 the Harlem Globetrotters were at the forefront of yet another broken barrier when Mannie Jackson, who had played for the team in the 1960s, bought the team. In doing so, he became the first African American owner of a major international sports/entertainment organization.

Lynette Woodard

In 1982 the Harlem Globetrotters became the only sports team ever honored with a star on the Hollywood Walk of Fame. The Hollywood Walk of Fame celebrates well-known entertainers of all kinds. In addition to their games on the court, there were two movies released about the team in the 1950s: *The Harlem Globetrotters* and *Go, Man, Go!* They also starred in TV shows, ranging from the *Harlem Globetrotters* Saturday morning cartoon in the 1970s and 1980s to *The Harlem Globetrotters Popcorn Machine* variety show in the 1970s. The team and its players have also appeared on shows like *Sesame Street*,

American Ninja Warrior, Little Big Shots, Mutt & Stuff, The Goldbergs, and *The Amazing Race.*

And you can also find the Harlem Globetrotters at the Naismith Memorial Basketball Hall of Fame. Not only have a number of people associated with the Globetrotters been inducted, the team itself was inducted in 2002. They became only the fifth team to receive that honor.

Harlem Globetrotters in the
Basketball Hall of Fame:

Wilt Chamberlain

Zachary Clayton

Nathaniel "Sweetwater" Clifton

William "Pop" Gates

Connie Hawkins

Elvin Hayes

Marques Haynes

Mannie Jackson

Meadowlark Lemon

Abe Saperstein

Reece "Goose" Tatum

Lynette Woodard

CHAPTER 3
Going Global

After the Harlem Globetrotters became a sensation in the United States, they set their sights on the rest of the world. Today, with global air travel, streaming video, social media, and websites, nearly every US sports league has plenty of fans overseas. But back in the 1940s, sports were still very much local or regional. That changed in the early 1950s when Saperstein planned the first trip across the Atlantic Ocean by an organized basketball team. The Globetrotters visited countries in Europe and Africa on their first world tour.

The stops in Europe were important for reasons that reached beyond basketball. At that time the Cold War was beginning to rage. The Cold War wasn't a war in the traditional sense—no soldiers fought on battlegrounds. But it was a period of dangerously strained relations between the United States and the Soviet Union. (The Soviet Union was a huge country that included today's Russia, Ukraine, Kazakhstan, and twelve other nations.) The threat of real war was constant, all the way through the 1980s.

The Globetrotters waded into this fray on August 22, 1951, when they played a game in Berlin, Germany. At that time Germany was divided into West Germany (aligned with the United States) and East Germany (aligned with the Soviet Union). Seventy-five thousand people came to Olympic Stadium in the western part of Berlin to see the Globetrotters play that day— the largest crowd the Harlem Globetrotters ever played for, even to this day! To put that size in perspective, when a basketball game is sold out at New York's Madison Square Garden, about nineteen thousand people fill the stands. Almost four times that amount came to Olympic Stadium!

The team ventured even deeper into Cold War territory later in the 1950s. As part of a tour of the Soviet Union and Eastern Europe, the Globetrotters played their first game in Moscow in August 1959. Among the players who made the trip: basketball legend Wilt Chamberlain, who still holds the record for most points scored during a single NBA game—one hundred!

Wilt Chamberlain

On their second world tour, in 1952, Secretary of State Dean Acheson, the US government official in charge of foreign policy, publicly praised the Globetrotters as "ambassadors of goodwill," a role they have continued to embrace. In 2013 they became one of the handful of US organizations of any kind to visit North Korea, a country that is isolated from much of the rest of the world.

The team has met with many world political and religious leaders through the years, including Nelson Mandela (a political activist who became the first black president of South Africa) and several popes. Nelson Mandela, Pope John Paul II,

The team with Nelson Mandela

and Pope Francis are among the ten people named Honorary Harlem Globetrotters, a title designed

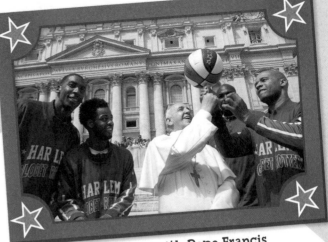

The team with Pope Francis

to acknowledge individuals "who have made an everlasting mark on the world." The others include political and religious leaders (former United States Secretary of State Dr. Henry Kissinger and Reverend Jesse Jackson), entertainers and TV personalities (Bob Hope, Whoopi Goldberg, and Robin Roberts), and athletes (Kareem Abdul-Jabbar and Jackie Joyner-Kersee).

The team with Robin Roberts

CHAPTER 4
Today and Days to Come

Now in their tenth decade, the Harlem Globetrotters show no signs of slowing down. They have played nearly twenty-seven thousand games since 1926. In 2016–2017, their ninetieth season, they played more than four hundred fifty games for about two million fans around the world. By comparison, every NBA team plays eighty-two games per season. That's 368 more chances to see the Harlem Globetrotters play!

2017 also marked two big milestones for the team: seventy-five years of the Harlem Globetrotters playing games for and entertaining the US military and the sixty-fifth year that the song "Sweet Georgia Brown" was used as their official theme song.

Unlike many attractions that were popular in 1926, like the Ringling Brothers and Barnum & Bailey Circus (which disbanded in May 2017), the Globetrotters are still going strong. The team posts game highlights, fan interactions, and behind-the-scenes footage on social media, where it has millions of followers.

In addition to traveling around the world, the Globetrotters have played in every kind of venue, from baseball stadiums to skate parks, inside mountains, on ice, and on aircraft carriers. They've used a glow-in-the-dark ball to play in the dark. They've sent a game ball into outer space on Space Shuttle *Atlantis*, and it returned to Earth with Harlem Globetrotters' team mascot, Globie, who parachuted it down from high above. That ball now lives at the Naismith Memorial Basketball Hall of Fame.

Is there anywhere the Globetrotters haven't been? Yes! There's one place where the Globetrotters have never played: Antarctica. Maybe someday they'll play for a crowd of penguins!

The Globetrotters have been basketball innovators as well, unveiling a four-point line thirty feet from the basket (or about six feet farther away than the NBA's three-point arc). And they've broken records: past and current Globetrotters currently hold sixteen Guinness World Records, including Longest Blindfolded Basketball Hook Shot and Farthest Basketball Shot Made While Sitting on the Court.

What's next for this team? Come on—the Globetrotters aren't going to spoil the surprise! But you can bet that it'll be a whole lot of fun for both the players and their millions of fans!

EXPERT

HISTORY
OF FUN STUFF

EXPERT
ON THE

HARLEM
GLOBETROTTERS

Congratulations! You've come to the end of this book. You're now an official History of Fun Stuff Expert on the Harlem Globetrotters. Go ahead and impress your friends and family with all the cool things you know about this incredible basketball team. And the next time you watch the Harlem Globetrotters play a game, you can remember all the amazing things you learned about them!

Hey, kids! Now that you're an expert on the history of the Harlem Globetrotters, turn the page to learn even more about earth science, geography, and basketball history (plus how to make a time line).

Basketball Time Line

Time lines show how something unfolded from the earliest date to the latest date. Below is a time line of some of the major events in the history of basketball from its beginning in 1891 to the present day.

History of Basketball

(1891)
Basketball is invented by a Canadian physical education teacher, James Naismith. The first game is played in Springfield, Massachusetts, where Naismith lived at the time.

1890   1900   1910   1920   1930   1940

(1936)
Basketball becomes an official Olympic sport at the summer games in Berlin, Germany. The United States team beats the team from Canada 19-8.

(1949)
In the early days of professional basketball there were many different leagues in the United States. In this year two of them merge to form the NBA (National Basketball Association).

Now that you've looked at this time line, do you think you could make a time line of the history of the Harlem Globetrotters using this book as a guide? Take out a clean sheet of paper. Let's start with the year the Globetrotters were founded, which is 1926. Since 1926 is our first date, let's start the time line in 1920 and make equal segments from 1920-1940, 1940-1960, and so on until we get to 2000-2020. You should have five segments on your line with each segment representing twenty years. Now read this book again and add in important Harlem Globetrotters dates to your time line.

1950   1960   1970   1980   1990   2000   2010

(1950)
The NBA's color barrier is broken and African American players are recruited for NBA teams.

(1997)
The WNBA (Women's National Basketball Association) holds its first game, although women had been playing the sport since its very beginnings in the 1890s.

(1968)
The Naismith Memorial Basketball Hall of Fame opens its doors in Springfield, Massachusetts, although it was founded in 1959.

(2003)
Michael Jordan, perhaps the greatest basketball player ever, retires. Throughout his career, he led the Chicago Bulls to six NBA championships.

All About Antarctica

The Harlem Globetrotters have traveled all over the world, but the one place they haven't played is Antarctica. Antarctica is the world's southernmost continent, and most of it is covered in ice. Here are nine facts about Antarctica!

• Antarctica is covered in so much ice that most of the world's freshwater (about 70 percent) is frozen there. Freshwater is the kind of water humans can drink. Saltwater is the kind we can't.

• Even though Antarctica is covered in ice, it hardly ever rains or snows, making Antarctica a desert!

• The only people who live in Antarctica live in scientific research stations owned by different countries. Depending on the time of year, one thousand to four thousand people live at these stations.

• During its winter most parts of Antarctica get no sunlight.

• During its summer Antarctica has no night. It's daylight twenty-four hours a day.

• Emperor penguins live in Antarctica in large colonies, or groups.

• In 2010 the coldest temperature on Earth was recorded on Antarctica. It was -135.8 degrees Fahrenheit.

• Antarctica is the fifth largest out of the seven continents. It's about the size of the United States (minus Alaska and Hawaii) plus another half of the United States.

• If all the ice on Antarctica melted, the oceans around the world would rise two hundred feet.

Basketball Around the World

Basketball might have originated in the United States, but today it is popular all over the world. Because of the sport's popularity outside of the US, every year the Harlem Globetrotters embark on a world tour. And that's not all. In the 2016 Olympics in Rio de Janiero, Brazil, twelve countries competed for gold in both men's and women's

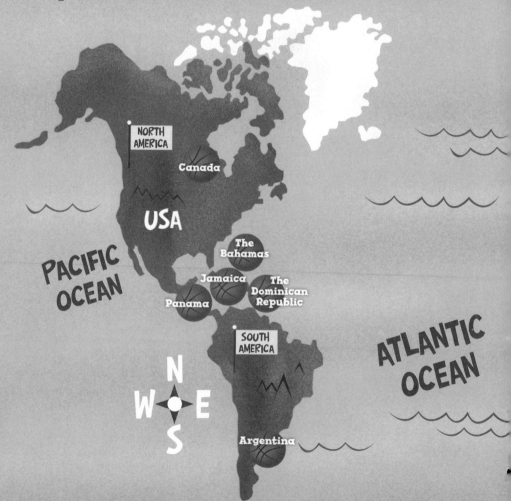

basketball. In both events the USA won the gold medal.

In the NBA there are a number of players who come from places other than the United States. Players have come from countries such as Argentina, Australia, the Bahamas, Canada, China, Croatia, the Dominican Republic, France, Germany, Greece, Jamaica, Lithuania, the Netherlands, Nigeria, Panama, Serbia, Spain, and Sudan.

Being an expert on something means you can get an awesome score on a quiz on that subject! Take this

History of the Harlem Globetrotters Quiz

to see how much you've learned.

1. In what decade were the Harlem Globetrotters formed?
   a. 1920s
   b. 1960s
   c. 2000s

2. Who was the first female Harlem Globetrotter?
   a. TNT Lister
   b. Ace Jackson
   c. Lynette Woodard

3. On which television show have the Harlem Globetrotters appeared?
   a. *Sesame Street*
   b. *SpongeBob SquarePants*
   c. *Mr. Rogers' Neighborhood*

4. How far is the four-point line from the basket?
   a. 2 feet
   b. 30 feet
   c. 1 mile

5. Which continent was not on the Harlem Globetrotters' first world tour in 1950?
   a. Europe
   b. Africa
   c. Antarctica

6. How many people saw the Harlem Globetrotters play on August 22, 1951?
   a. 15,000
   b. 1 million
   c. 75,000

7. Why was "Harlem" incorporated into the team name?
   a. because of the popularity of the Harlem Renaissance
   b. because the team was from New York City
   c. because the team played their first game in Harlem

8. How did a Harlem Globetrotters basketball go into outer space?
   a. It was thrown up there.
   b. It traveled on the Space Shuttle *Atlantis*.
   c. It never went into outer space.

Answers: 1.a 2.c 3.a 4.b 5.c 6.c 7.a 8.b